America's Chessboard

America's Chessboard

...

James Herschel Taylor

No aspect of this book may be used or reproduced by any means, including but not limited to the following: graphic, electronic, or mechanical.

Photocopying, recording, taping, or any action taken to illegally reproduce this manuscript's contents by any information storage retrieval system without the written permission of the author/publisher, except in the case of brief quotations embodied in critical articles and reviews, is forbidden.

© 2016 James Herschel Taylor
All rights reserved.

ISBN: 0989095762
ISBN: 9780989095761
Library of Congress Control Number: 2016908073
New Writers In Action, Havre De Grace, MD

Cover Design by Gerald Norris Jr.
Art Design by Minuteman Press

To my parents, James and Berhonda Taylor

*In loving memory of my Grandmother (Nana),
Luevnia Williams Taylor
7/08/1931 to 5/23/2016*

Also to Ms. Millie, my mentor.

"To all people around the world, and my Creator."

Join James Herschel Taylor in his journey to an understanding of his true feelings as he develops into a published author.

Table of Contents

Foreword · ix

Preface The Beginning to My Arrival · · · · · · · · · · · xi

Introduction · xxix

Chapter 1   The Kings and Queens · 1

Chapter 2   The Rooks · 19

Chapter 3   The Bishops · 28

Chapter 4   The Knights · 36

Chapter 5   Pawn One: The Native Americans · · · · · · · · · · · · · · · 55

Chapter 6   Pawn Two: The White Americans · · · · · · · · · · · · · · · 70

Chapter 7   Pawn Three: The Hispanic Americans · · · · · · · · · · 77

Chapter 8   Pawn Four: The Asian Americans · · · · · · · · · · · · · · 83

Chapter 9 Pawn Five: The Afro-Americans · · · · · · · · · · · · · · ·90

Chapter 10 The Overview · 103

The Conclusion · 105

Book Club Discussion and Topics · · · · · · · · · · · · · 109

Notes · 111

Foreword

• • •

FIRST, I MUST GIVE ALL honor, glory, and praise to the Most High God, Yah, for blessing my son with this opportunity and idea to write his book, *America's Chessboard*, and for bringing such a wonderful mentor, Ms. Millie McGhee-Morris, into our son's life.

James's father, James Irving Taylor, and I would like to congratulate our son on his very first book. We are so very proud of him. We've always told him that he had a God-given purpose in life and to always be true to himself. This would be the most important thing he could do in life: stay true to self.

Even before our son was conceived, my husband and I discussed at length how we were going to raise him. I had a vision from the Most High God, Yah, that we would be having a son. Yah showed me our son as a toddler even before he was conceived. We decided we would raise our son to be a God-fearing child who loves and respects the word of Yah and Yah's people. We discussed how he should treat himself and others as well. Our son, James, is loving, kind, smart, self-motivated, polite, caring, and respectful toward us as his parents as well as others.

Our son, James, has truly been an inspiration to us as his parents because of his drive to follow his passion about studying and finding his biblical Hebrew Israelite ancestors. He is dedicated to educating African Americans about finding their Hebrew ancestors. We are inspired and encouraged by his enthusiasm to reach his goals. He taught us how to conduct research to find out where our Hebrew ancestors fit in our family tree. This has given us a sense of pride as African Americans. I pray that everyone who reads this book will feel our son's passion and be inspired.

Berhonda F. Taylor
Mother of author James Herschel
Taylor

Preface
The Beginning to My Arrival

• • •

MY PARENTS, JAMES AND BERHONDA Taylor, told me that they planned for my arrival even before I was conceived. They talked about how I was going to be raised all the way down to what I was going to eat.

My parents met at the ages of thirty-five on a blind date set up by their mutual best friends, who were married at the time. My future dad got there early (with flowers) to beat my future mom there so that he could check her out first, just in case he had to make an exit through the back door.

Fortunately, it was love at first sight for my future dad and mom. They told me they knew on that first blind date at Chantilly's Cafe in Alton, Illinois, that they were going to get married. My dad said he took one look into my mom's eyes, and it was a done deal—he knew at that time they were going to get married. My mom told me that it was a magical, beautiful, and romantic blind date and courtship. My mom said that dating my dad was her best dating experience ever! My dad said that after one month of dating my mom, he said to her, "Girl, you are going to make me marry you!" They dated for one year almost to the exact day from their first date. When this was told to me, I thought, "I almost didn't happen because my mom was preparing to move back home to Arkansas right before she met my dad. However, she decided to give this blind date a chance first—wow!" They were married on June 5, 1998, in the rose garden at Gordon Moore Park in Alton, Illinois. They were both thirty-six years of age and bought a home in a quiet subdivision in Alton.

My mom said had she'd known that Alton, IL, was one of the most haunted places in America, she wouldn't have moved there if she'd had a choice. However, it seemed love won her over. Mom said she had a vision of having a little baby boy wearing blue denim overalls.

My mom only wanted to have a son, but my dad actually assumed she would have a daughter first because during that time our family was mostly girls. However, during the time of the testing to see if I was a girl or boy, I was told that I kept my parents in suspense by keeping my legs crossed until the eighth month of my mom's pregnancy. Then, during another ultrasound, I finally showed my parents that I was a boy. My dad was still in disbelief, but both of my parents were filled with so much joy.

So, needless to say, when I was born on August 16, 1999 (six days before my mother's thirty-seventh birthday), both my father—who wouldn't let anyone except my mom and the nurses touch me because he was extremely protective—and mother were elated, and my mother's vision had come to pass.

My aunt, my father's sister, was at the hospital after my birth and told my parents that I would become a great speaker and leader and that people would come from all around the world to hear me speak. I also have had other aunts in Arkansas pray and prophesize the very same thing about my future throughout my very young life.

During the first four years of my life, I was very ill because, as my pediatrician told my parents, my lungs were not quite developed. They had to deliver me early by C-section because my mom was a first-time older parent and because of the delivery risks that came with her age. My parents had to take me to the doctor on an average of every two weeks until I turned four years old.

My parents and I went to the doctors so much that whenever we visited the pharmacist, they would say, "Here comes that singer James Taylor again!" Believe me, I'm no singer! My parents took turns sleeping with me in their bed as I was recovering from my illness to be able to monitor my serious respiratory conditions. This was the only way my parents could take turns getting sleep to be able to go and perform their duties at their respective jobs. My mom became a distributor of Juice Plus, and for approximately three years, I took all-natural fruit-and-vegetable gummies every day. This, along with much prayer, was the beginning of my healing.

My parents took many pictures of me with a knot on my head on almost every birthday photo because I was an active and energetic toddler. I was always running (and running into something), especially on my birthday before my first birthday photo was taken—almost like clockwork—every year.

My parents said I was a very smart and independent child who had a love for history at a very young age. Like any other child, I had to be encouraged to be more obedient because as Mom always said, "Obedience is better than sacrifice!"

My parents have a toddler photo of me taking out the rolling trash-cans (which were larger and taller than I was) to the end of the driveway so that our trash could be picked up the next morning. I enjoyed helping my parents with chores around our home.

I remember my mom being consistently and daily in prayer, reading her Bible, or praying with or for someone in need. Mom really enjoyed praying. At a very young age, I would pray with her as she prayed for others. My dad said he remembers waking up in the early hours of the morning to go to the bathroom, and as he was walking through my toddler bedroom, my dad said that I had my hands in the praying position, praying for my Uncle Wayne.

I learned through the research of my Hebrew heritage faith that the actual name of my God is Yah, as written in Psalm 68:4: "Sing unto God, sing praises to his name: extol him that rideth upon the heavens by his name Jah (Yah), and rejoice before him." The letter "J" was not in existence until the 1600s. The New Testament was translated from Greek, and the Old Testament was translated from Hebrew and Aramaic text. During the translation of the King James version, God's original name was changed from "Yah" to "Jah" in the King James Version Bible.[1]

---

1 https://en.wikipedia.org/wiki/King_James_Version.

My mom says that I am an anointed child who is called and chosen by my Creator, to do my life's work according to His will. My dad believes this also. To this day, at the age of sixteen, I love and enjoy praying and reading my Bible daily. I was even led by Yah to get rid of my game console to obtain a closer walk with Yah. I have several Bibles and history books, and a plethora of ancient photos of archaeological artifacts about my Hebrew heritage, which I will discuss more later on.

In the third grade, I was diagnosed with Asperger's, which is a milder form of autism, which really comes in handy for making excellent grades in school. My parents were surprised when I was diagnosed with Asperger's. After much research, my parents found out the Asperger's gene comes from the father's side. My dad has Asperger's also but didn't know it until I was diagnosed. My dad said when he was in school, all they did back then was put you in special education, and no testing was ever done to diagnose anything. My dad had to get his mother, Luevnia, my grandmother, to fight with the school system and test my dad to get my dad out of special education, which eventually happened when he was in middle school. My dad is very smart, especially in math. As my mom puts it, "Your father has one thousand talents and uses every one of them!" I feel very fortunate to have a father who understands what I go through in life, living with Asperger's. My dad was able to reach and teach me on a level that no other teacher or person could.

My dad and I both having Asperger's has brought our relationship closer than I could have ever imagined. I thank Yah, the Most High Elohim, every day for my wonderful parents. They mean the world to me. They say I am a gift from Yah, the Most High Elohim, to them, but I say my parents are a gift from Yah, the Most High Elohim, to me.

I had my share of "bullies," to hear my mom and dad say it. It started, as my parents say, "from birth," dealing with a bad babysitter (whom my parents fired) and dealing with bad and aggressive kids at daycare, elementary, and middle school. I was a quiet kid who just loved to pray, read the Bible, and read history books. At the age of four, my parents put me in martial arts and later in

Capoeira to learn how to obtain more self-confidence, focus, and self-control and to protect myself, and it worked. Usually kids with Asperger's do better in individual sports rather than team sports. I later joined the chess club at my high school, Alton High, and have really enjoyed learning how to play chess. I have improved my skills and learned new strategies for beating my opponents at school. It is so much fun! I sometimes get beaten also, which humbles me and makes me work even harder. I play chess online to challenge myself more. I really enjoy my friends at Alton High. My friends have been very supportive of my interest in genealogy.

During my sophomore year, when my *Genealogy Roadshow* segment aired on television, my German teacher, Frau Wimp, showed my German class my segment of the show. I was excited with joy when all my fellow students clapped for me at the end of my show.

I was named after my father, James Taylor, and my grandfather, Herschel Watson. I have my father's first name, James, and my grandfather's first name, Herschel, as my middle name. Thus, my name is James Herschel Taylor. My parents' say that I look like my father and act like both my father and grandfather. I also picked up some of my talents from my dad, being peaceful and creative, being smart, having a love of fishing, being a hard worker, and being pretty good in math.

I picked up my mother's outgoing personality (learned behavior taught to me by my mom), persistence, positive energy, talent for writing, and love of prayer, the Bible, and history. The talents I picked up from my grandfather are his love of God, his charisma, and his very good athletic skills. My grandmother, my dad's mom, Luevnia, told my parents before I was conceived that she just wanted to live to see me be born, and now she is eighty-four years of age with a fighting spirit. I inherited her fighting spirit. I admire my grandmother Luevnia because she raised eight children and fought hard to keep her family together and safe through prayer.

I have many other relatives who have played a major part in the spiritual and positive development of my life. I have four aunts (who all have master's degrees) on my mother's side, who are my four godmothers. Aunt T. T., Teresia Dupins, is a co-pastor, minister, and author and one of my prayer warriors, supporters, and encouragers. With her knowledge of the medical field, she kept me on course with my physical and mental development, along with her husband, my uncle Prentice Dupins Sr., who is a pastor, teacher of thirty years (now retired), writer, and film director. He's always been very supportive and prayed for me. Aunt K. K., Phyllis Rice, has been a teacher for twenty-seven years and was named 2008–2009 Teacher of the Year for McKinley Elementary School in California. She influenced me most in my college choices, she helped me to think outside of the box and learn to laugh out loud, and she supported, encouraged, and prayed for me, along with her late husband, my uncle Darrell Rice. He was an engineer for the Los Angeles County Fire Department before he passed away April 22, 2014, from a fire-related illness. I miss him dearly—he was also very supportive and encouraging. Aunt Shelia, Herschelia Watson, is a program coordinator for at-risk youth. She prayed for me, encouraged and supported me with her great social worker skills, and taught my parents about resources that were available to me since I have Asperger's. Lastly I have

Aunt Gigi, Jenny Watson, an administrator who kept me laughing and helped me to stay on course by using her skills in psychology and teaching me how to communicate with others along with praying for me and encouraging me.

I also have a second cousin, Mrs. Carolyn Coclough, an evangelist who is like an aunt to me—I even call her "Aunt Carol." She was one of my prayer warriors and was my biggest encourager and supporter when it came to researching my DNA, which led me to finding out my genealogy. Finding my true heritage set me on the path to making one of the most important changes in my life, which was my walk with Yah, the Most High Elohim. I know that I am of the chosen Hebrew people of Yah, the Most High Elohim, which is written in Genesis through Deuteronomy, the first five books of the Bible.

The search for my DNA to be profiled and my family's genealogy to be researched began when I was eight years of age. I questioned my mother and father about my family's genealogy, and my mother put me in contact with my second cousin, whom I fondly call "Aunt Carol," and my first cousin, Amanda Dupins. They both gave me all the information that they had researched, which set me on my journey to finding my roots on my mother's side. Then I wanted to know about my father's side of the family, but my father had never known or seen his biological father, so he only could direct me to my grandmother Luevnia to find out more information. I kept on bugging my mom, telling her that I wanted my DNA profiled done very badly. My mom told me, just as I asked, she turned and look at the television, and there was the information about the *Genealogy Roadshow*, and then the Holy Spirit led my mom to apply for me to be on the show.

My mom entered my photo and story to the *Genealogy Roadshow*, and I was picked within two weeks of applying online. We found out later from the genealogist who had picked me that he was drawn to me because I reminded him of himself at that age. I became the first child at the age of fourteen to be chosen to be on the second season of the *Genealogy Roadshow*, which aired on January 20, 2015.

The *Genealogy Roadshow* did something so wonderful for me. They submitted my DNA and my dad's DNA to be analyzed, and they revealed my DNA results on the show. The results traced my family origins back to Mali, a country in West Africa. This confirmed all the research that I had done prior to the show's airing. How cool is that? Another great thing was that my dad found out who his dad and his dad's family were. It was extremely emotional for my dad and us as a family, but it was such a gift! The *Genealogy Roadshow* also gave me a very large and beautiful family-tree chart and all of the data used in the research of my genealogy. That day was the one of the best days of my young life! I was so happy—I never thought I could smile that hard. Now and in the future, I want to help and support people just like my parents do. They are always there for their families, friends, and even strangers. I have been blessed to have some wonderful mentors in my life. Through my Aunt K. K., Phyllis Rice, I met my first mentor, Tamela Tenpenny-Lewis, who's her sorority sister. When I met Mrs. Tenpenny-Lewis she was the national president of the AAHGS (Afro-American Historical and

Genealogical Society Inc.) My mom also met, Angela Parks-Pyles, the best friend of both Tamela and Aunt K. K. Angela found out that I was interested in genealogy and told my mom to contact Tamela Tenpenny-Lewis, who took me under her wing and had the Arkansas local AAHGS chapter members, friends, and sponsors pay for my mother and me to fly and stay in a hotel so that we could attend the National AAHGS Conference in Pennsylvania. At the conference, I was a youth-in-training as Mrs. Tenpenny assistant on Friday, October 10, 2014. I was chosen to be the moderator at the sharing dinner and got to introduce the keynote speaker, Tony Burroughs, the founder and CEO of the Center for Black Genealogy. I was the youngest person who attended the National AAHGS Conference that year, which was such an honor. At the conference, I also met another mentor, Professor Roland Barksdale-Hall, who is a faculty member in the Africana Studies Department at Youngstown State University. Professor Barksdale-Hall has encouraged me in my endeavors to be a university professor by sending me books of interest about the history of my heritage.

At the conference, I was also very fortunate to meet an awesome person who would later become my mentor, Ms. Millie McGhee-Morris, the CEO of New Writers in Action and the publisher of my first book, *America's Chessboard*. She said that I reminded her of herself when she was young. She has been extremely supportive and one of my biggest cheerleaders.

I can't express the dedication, patience, generosity, and time she's provided to help mold me into the writer she knows I'm capable of being. Her organization provides students the opportunity to achieve their dreams of becoming authors along with the benefit of awarding them a scholarship for college. In January 2016, Ms. Millie flew in to visit and shadow me during my communications class, where Ms. Macias was my teacher.

Ms. Millie was impressed with the way my teacher kept control of my class and how all of the students in my class behaved in an orderly and respectful manner. I appreciate Ms. Millie so very much, and I am extremely grateful to Yah for blessing me with the opportunity to have Ms. Millie in my life.

My aspirations are to please Yah, the Most High Elohim, and to live according to his will. I want to make my parents proud of me, to give back to others, to become a published author, and to obtain my doctorate in archeology with a minor in anthropology so that I can become a university professor.

I would like to thank every relative, family member, teacher, and person who has ever done anything to encourage, support, and shape my life into what Yah, the Most High Elohim, has ordained for me—for that I am very thankful and grateful.

Introduction

• • •

THROUGHOUT MY LIFE LIVING AS an American citizen in America, I've come to realize it's like living on a chessboard. You might ask, How is it like living on a chessboard? I have seen how the rich get richer, how the poor get poorer, and how the rich benefit more by manipulating the tax and business laws. On another level, race also plays a big role in this country, such as how police officers react differently to different races when confronting them and how the amount of time a person spends in jail may vary based on the racial majority of the jurors.

You might also be wondering which race is generally the poorest and which race is usually the richest. These questions can be answered based upon experience and statistics.

If there's a town that is all poor, there's going to be constant competition and high crime between everyone, and these competitions increase in intensity if there are multiple ethnic groups living in the same areas. An example of this would be the Hispanics and the Blacks in Los Angeles; there are constant racial tensions in these areas because most of these areas are poor. A lot of these tensions are due to the lack of jobs and lack of good education. Since America began with white supremacy and racism, it's going to end that same way.

CHAPTER 1

The Kings and Queens

• • •

The Kings and Queens represent the top 1 percent who can move in any number of vacant spaces. They have their own power and money.

THE REASON FOR WRITING THIS book is that I've always wanted to be of help to people. I enjoy genealogy; finding my roots inspired me to want to teach others in this world how to understand what really happened back in the days long ago. I feel the truth should be told so people won't be lost and in fear. What you fear is what you hate because fear is the progenitor of ignorance and hatred.

KINGS AND QUEENS

Throughout history, many nations have had their own kings and queens. This is called a monarchy. A monarchy is a government ruled by a king or a queen. This type of government is in many countries; this can be seen in England, parts of Asia, and parts of the Middle East. Who really controls this world? There is only one God, who we all know and revere, but that's religion.

I am talking about people who try to change the way this whole chess game is played. You might be wondering why I compare the world to a chessboard. I use it to make a comparison because in this world we do have kings, queens, bishops, knights, rooks, and pawns. The king usually is the one in power and who has the most control, such as a president or prime minister. The queen is usually second in power. The queen doesn't possess the same amount of power as the king, but she has similar powers. The bishop is the priest—or in this book, the one who controls religion. The rook is the siege engine use to carry the knight. The knight in this book is the law enforcement, otherwise known as the police. Lastly, you have the pawns. They are the lowest on the chessboard of life. They represent the middle class and the poor. The other chess pieces who are higher and above the pawns have a deep animosity toward them, and they ridicule the pawns. The pawns are the serfs—they are bound in debt—which have lower living conditions than the Kings and Queens, which means they have to pay a high price to be able to survive in this world. The pawns (serfs) also have to grow food and work for the nobles. Now, you might be asking yourself, "Why is the author giving us a lesson on medieval chess?" Well, reader, it's going to give you a better understanding of what I'm about to say. One of my own sayings is, "Money is like the blood that keeps the body going, physically and literally."

In America, there have been many powerful families who still have "old money" from the wealth their ancestors acquired. Their ancestors acquired money in many ways. One of those ways was the ownership of slaves (free labor). Another way the kings (the top 1 percent) stay in control and stay rich is by controlling energy, food, education, and healthcare.

The King

There are several families in America who are extremely rich. These families are actually the kings, who have enough money to rule the world and to negotiate with anyone. The kings tend to fund political systems through their queens.

The first family I would like to discuss is the Rothschild family. The Rothschilds are considered the richest family in the world. In 1760, Mayor Amschel Rothschild placed his five sons in the world's five financial centers. The family solidified its global reach in the nineteenth century by funding monarchies, governments, and both sides in the Napoleonic Wars. A newspaper at the time described the family as the brokers and counselors of the kings of Europe and the Republican chiefs of America. Today, the Rothschild family is said to maintain its control through the US Federal Reserve, having deployed its agent, Paul Warburg, to create the powerful quasigovernment entity in 1913.

In my research, my father told me to watch the movie *Thrive*.[2] He said it would help me understand who is in control in America. In watching *Thrive*, I learned that the Rothschilds control Bank of America.

---

2 *Thrive: What on Earth Will It Take?* Clear Compass Media, LLC.

The Rockefeller family empire began in 1870, when John D. Rockefeller founded the Standard Oil Company, which would make him the richest single person in history with a net worth of $400 billion. The Rockefellers control the ExxonMobil companies. The Rockefellers control America's food by large-scale petroleum-based agriculture. This began during the Green Revolution in the 1970s. They also make all the oil-based fertilizers. The American Medical Association is funded by the Rockefellers to influence research in medical practices. The Rockefellers control Citibank. Recognizing the threat of such wealth, President Theodore Roosevelt warned that the Rockefellers' interest was creating an invisible government. The Rockefeller plan has since included funding the United Nations headquarters and founding the Bilderberg Conferences of the global super elite. Today, the Rockefeller family continues its agenda through controlling interests in Chase Manhattan Bank, ExxonMobil, Chevron, and BP.

The next family to discuss is the Morgan Family. The Morgans ascended when John Pierpont Morgan and the Rothschilds gave the US Treasury 3.5 million ounces of gold during the Panic of

1893. Having control of the US gold supply, Morgan financed the creation of America's largest corporations, including GE, AT&T, and US Steel. This leverage over the US Treasury led to charges that the Morgan family forced America into World War I to protect loans made to Russia and France. J. P. Morgan Jr. provided a $500 million war loan and collected a 1 percent commission on the supplies his corporations provided. It is also rumored that the Morgans played a role in encouraging the Japanese attack on Pearl Harbor by conspiring to share war profits with the Iwaki and Dan clans, who owned Mitsubishi and Mitsui. Today the Morgan family maintains the world's largest private gold vault—allegedly linked by tunnel to the New York Federal Reserve Bank.

The Bush political dynasty began with Prescott Sheldon Bush, who was born in 1895 and attended Yale University as a member of the Skull and Bones Society (a symbol of the Masons). In 1933, it is rumored that Bush led a failed coup attempt against President FDR (funded by the DuPonts, Rockefellers, and Morgans) to install a fascist dictatorship in the United States. The business plot was covered up, and Bush rose to be the director of the Union

Banking Corporation when it was suspected of hiding Nazi gold during World War II. I understand that both Prescott's son, George H. W., and grandson, George W., became presidents of the United States, and both initiated wars with Iraq that profited companies with Bush family ties, such as Halliburton and KBR. Today the Bushes are considered the most powerful family in US politics, having significant fortunes in banking and oil and having yet another member, Jeb, running to be the next president, who has since withdrawn from the presidential race.

The last family I want to discuss is the Warburgs. In doing more research, I came across the website KingdomsoftheWorld.com,[3] which featured an article on the Warburg family. The Warburgs came on the scene in the sixteenth century. Known as Court Jews, they lived in the town of Warburg, which is between Frankfurt and Hamburg, which is how they got their name. At the time, German law did not allow Jewish families to have their own surnames, and it was forbidden to own land or perform everyday trades. Thus, the Jews developed the trade of handling of money. They loaned money at interest and dealt in

---
3 kingdomsoftheworld.com.

foreign exchange. Money made up for the stigma placed on the Warburgs. The Christian society would only let the Warburgs pursue the money trade. Being in this role made the Warburgs feel withdrawn and disliked. The Warburg family moved to Hamburg in the seventeenth century and became international bankers. Hamburg became Germany's principal port due to their alliance.

M. M. Warburg and Company grew as a private bank. By 1914, M. M. Warburg became the leading German commercial bank established on Wall Street. Felis M. Warburg and his brother, Paul, masterminded the foundation of an American central bank, the Federal Reserve, in 1913.

Rothschild used, The Federal Reserve Bank, Rockefeller, and Morgan families to bail themselves out through taxes (IRS). Who, you might ask, plays the most crucial role in the US economy? It's the Federal Reserve. Most people do not know what the Federal Reserve does or how it impacts people in their everyday lives. They are sometimes called the "Fed." Who is the gatekeeper of the US economy? The Fed. The Fed is based in Washington, DC as the bank of the United States. There are twelve Federal Reserve banks and a number of branches in this network. The Board of Governors supervises the Federal Reserve Bank. The Fed can make decisions on its own without requiring approval from any other branch of government—except it can be questioned by Congress over its actions. The president nominates the Fed board members, and the Senate must approve them.

Speaking of kings, here's a list of fifteen major companies that have admitted their companies have profited from having links to slavery:

J. P. MORGAN CHASE, 1831–1865

The research reported that two of their predecessor banks, Citizens Bank and Canal Bank in Louisiana, received approximately 13,000 enslaved people as collateral on loans and took ownership of approximately 1,250 of them when plantation owners failed to pay the loans back.

Lehman Brothers, Civil War

The Lehman brothers' business empire started in the slave trade, and, according to research, they recently admitted their part in the business of slavery.

According to the *Sun Times*,[4] this firm admitted that during the Civil War, their founding partners owned and profited from slavery.

Aetna Inc., 1853

Aetna is one the largest health insurer in the United States. Aetna acknowledged the part they played in insuring the lives of slaves to reimburse slave owners for losses when a slave died.

New York Life, 1847

In the United States, New York Life Insurance Company is the largest mutual life insurance company. According to *USA Today*,[5] proof of ten more New York Life slave policies comes from an account book that contained notes by a Natchez, Mississippi, agent, W. A. Britton, on slave policies for the amounts ranging from

---

4 *Sun Times.*
5 *USA Today.*

$375 to $600. According to the 1906 history of the company's first 1,000 policies, 339 policies were written on slaves.

WACHOVIA CORPORATION (NOW OWNED BY WELLS FARGO)

According to *USA Today*,[6] it was disclosed that two of the Wachovia Corporation's predecessors owned enslaved Africans and received slaves as payment.

N.M. ROTHSCHILD AND SONS BANK IN LONDON, NINETEENTH CENTURY

An article in the *Financial Times*[7] disclosed that Nathan Mayer Rothschild, the banking family's patriarch, profited first personally by using slaves as collateral in business dealings with slave owners.

THE MOBILE AND GIRARD COMPANY (NOW PART OF NORFOLK SOUTHERN)

As written on AtlantaBlackStar.com,[8] Norfolk Southern gave the slave owners $180 (which is equivalent to $3,379 today) per person

---
6 Ibid.
7 *Financial Times*.
8 Atlantablackstar.com.

for slaves they rented to the railroad for one year. The Central of Georgia, another company joined with Norfolk Southern today, valued their slaves at $31,303 (equivalent to $663,033 today) on record.

USA TODAY, (PARENT COMPANY, E. W. SCRIPPS AND GANNETT)

USA Today[9] found out their parent company had had connections to the slave trade.

FLEETBOSTON (FROM PROVIDENCE BANK)

John Brown, who was the founder of Providence Bank, traded slaves. He also owned ships that were used to transport slaves. This bank financed Brown's voyages to obtain slaves, and the bank profited from slaves. Brown even reportedly helped charter what later became Brown University.

CSX

More than a century ago, the political and legal system that was in place allowed CSX to use slave labor to construct portions of the

---

9 *USA Today.*

US rail lines. The cost of slaves to rent for a season was up to $200 (the equivalent of $3,800 today).

The Canadian National Railway Company (Now Part of the Mobile and Ohio)

This company is a headquartered in Montreal, Quebec, and serves Canada and the midwestern and southern United States. They are a class 1 Canadian railway. They profited from slavery and valued their slaves lost to the war and emancipation at $199,691 on record, which is equivalent to a current value of $2.2 million.

Brown Brothers Harriman, 1818

Brown Brothers Harriman is the oldest and largest private investment bank and securities firm in the United States. *USA Today* reported that the New York merchant bank of James and William Brown, currently known as Brown Brothers Harriman, financed the cotton economy, lending millions to southern planters, merchants, and cotton brokers. They also owned hundreds of slaves.

Brooks Brothers, 1800s

This retailer's beginning came from selling clothing made for slaves to various slave traders.

Barclays (Headquartered in London, United Kingdom)

This British multinational banking and financial services company admitted they bought companies that may have been involved in slave trade.

AIG—New York–Based Company (Purchased American General Financial Group, the Houston-Based Insurer That Owns US Life Insurance Company)

In 1935, the *American Conservationist Magazine*[10] printed an article indicating that a life insurance policy was written on a slave living in Kentucky.

---

10 *The American Conservationist Magazine.*

The Queens

As stated earlier, the queen is second in power and has similar powers as the king. One of the top positions in America (and in the world) is the president. The president is considered to be in the queen position only because he has to get funding from Congress in order to fund his programs, which are usually approved by Congress. The kings control the political process in America because of the wealth they possess. The kings need a political atmosphere to help them stay in power.

Below are some of the queens in America. Their power is undeniable according to *Forbes* in their article "The World's Billionaires List,"[11] dated March 2, 2015. The following list of billionaires has extended to a record 1,826, including 290 more new billionaires on the scene since the report was published. Some of these billionaires may have political power; some may not.

Number one on the list is Bill Gates—he has kept this position sixteen out of the past twenty-one years.

---

11 "The World's Billionaires." *Forbes.com*. http://www.forbes.com/billionaires/list/.

Number two—Warren Buffett

Number three—Amancio Ortega

Some of the companies on the queen list are Microsoft, Facebook, Walmart, other Silicon Valley tech companies, Uber, and Theranos.

According to the *Policy Mic*,[12] *Tampa Bay Times*,[13] and PolitiFact.com,[14] some of the billionaires listed below play a role as donors in the following political parties.

Democrat donors: Warren Buffet, Tom Steyer, Michael Bloomberg, and George Soros. Republican donors: David and Charles Koch, Rupert Murdoch, S. Daniel Abraham, and Vincent McMahon.

Right-Wing donors: Sheldon Adelson.

---

12 *Policy Mic.*
13 *Tampa Bay Times.*
14 Politifact.com.

There are more queens, but many remain anonymous donors. Some queens have been known to play on different sides to push the support for their own agendas.

I grew up learning in school that the government is "for the people and by the people," but I have since found out that it's "for the money and by the money."

CHAPTER 2

The Rooks

• • •

IN EVERY NATION THERE IS a rook. You might be wondering, "What's a rook?" A rook is the third chess piece in chess. The word "rook" comes from the Persian word *rukh*. The word *rukh* means, "chariot," but you probably want me to get to the point. Essentially it's a castle. The castle is made to protect the king and queen. In some instances, there is only one ruler, and many nations throughout this world have their own form of a rook or castle. The rook can be seen as government agencies that protect the kings and queens, such as the FBI, the CIA, and the judicial courts. Many people throughout the years have stepped out of line, either by what they have said or what they have done. Some of those people have been taken out by means of assassination or assassination-for-hire. Some people have been tortured. Some people have been kidnapped and are missing, never to be seen again by their family and friends. The main goal for the rook is to protect the kings and queens, but if the kings and queens feel that their power, money, and agenda are threatened by a person, group, organization, or country, then the action is taken seriously, and that king and queen will devise a plan to remove that threat.

For example, as posted on the Internet by *CNN Wire*,[15] dated April 16, 2015, over two thousand Walmart employees were surprised when they were informed on Monday, April 16, 2015, that five stores were going to be temporarily closed for approximately six months due to plumbing problems that required extensive repairs. These five Walmart stores were located in Florida, Oklahoma, California, and Texas. An underlying threat that may have led to that situation, one employee felt, was that in 2012 some of the workers in one of the Walmart store locations led one of the first Black Friday protests.[16]

---

15 *CNN Wire*.
16 *CNN Wire*, "Why Walmart Abruptly Closed 5 Stores, Leaving 2,200 Employees out of Work," *Fox4KC.com*, last modified April 16, 2015. www.fox4kc.com/2015/04/16/why-walmart-abruptly-closed-5-stores-leaving-2200-employees-out-of-work/.

An article on the Internet, dated January 22, 2015 and entitled "Everyday Money: The Economy," listed five companies that laid off thousands of workers. The following is a listing of these companies, the number of workers who were laid off, and the reasons for these massive layoffs.

SCHLUMBERGER: NINE THOUSAND JOBS—AN OILFIELD SERVICES COMPANY

Despite strong fourth-quarter results, they laid off nine thousand employees worldwide in late 2014 when profits decreased and the demand for oil was reduced.

BAKER HUGHES AND HALLIBURTON: EIGHT THOUSAND JOBS—ENERGY COMPANIES THAT MERGED

With regard to energy companies ending strongly by year end, Baker Hughes laid off seven thousand employees, and Halliburton laid off one thousand employees when the prices fell for crude oil and gas.

American Express: Four Thousand Jobs—Global Services Company

Since failing to meet the long-term revenue increase goal that was targeted for the company, American Express reduced cost by laying off four thousand employees.

eBay: Twenty-Four Hundred Jobs—Online Shopping and Auction Website

The reason for the twenty-four hundred eBay employees being laid off included unfilled job positions, lackluster holiday sales, and decreased revenue.[17]

The first rook I will talk about is the FBI, which was established 106 years ago on July 26, 1908. It was first known as the Bureau of Investigation (BOI). An attorney general by the name of Bonaparte used the Department of Justice expense funds, which allowed him to hire thirty-four people to be in the BOI. The funds also came from veterans of the Secret Service. The FBI's main purpose is to protect and defend the United States

---

17 Brad Tuttle, "Why These Five Companies Are Laying Off Thousands of Workers," *Time.com*, Last modified January 22, 2015. www.time.com/money/3678511/ebay-amex-baker-hughes-layoffs/.

against terrorists and foreign intelligence threats and to support and enforce criminal laws in America. They provide leadership and criminal justice services to federal, state, municipal, and international agencies.

The FBI employs thirty-five thousand people, including special agents and professionals such as language interpreters, information gatherers, and so on. The FBI needs these people with these particular skill types so they can have an easier time locating terrorists, speaking in a foreign languages to foreign-intelligence spies, and gathering information quickly, effectively, and efficiently.

The second rook is the CIA. The CIA started sixty-seven years ago on September 18, 1947. The main purpose of this organization is to create a clearinghouse to spy on foreign governments and to collect information on foreign intelligence. In the CIA, there are five executive offices.

1. The Executive Office of the CIA supports the US military by gathering useful information.

2. The Directorate of Analysis produces intelligence investigations on key foreign and intercontinental issues of powerful and sometimes antigovernment sensitive topics.
3. The Directorate of Science and Technology, one of the four branches, enables tactical operations by analyzing and writing long-term strategic assessments.
4. The Directorate of Intelligence is comprised of thirteen offices created to support intelligence analysis missions. Six offices inspect broad transnational issues, four offices concentrate on regional, political, and economic issues, and three offices work on policy, collection, and staff support. The CIA's Directorate of Intelligence (DI) is on the forefront of protecting the United States' national security interests in a fast-changing world. As a DI analyst, the challenge is to anticipate and quickly assess rapidly evolving international developments and their impact, both positive and negative, on US policy concerns. Technological advances have increased the complexity, scope, and speed of potential risks to our national security; threats can come from farther away,

faster, and with less warning than ever before. Today, the CIA is an independent organization that is responsible for providing national security intelligence for senior US policymakers. The president—with the advice and consent of the senate—nominates the director of the Central Intelligence Agency (D/CIA).[18]

American history has shown how rooks handled the following people when they posed a threat to a king's or queen's agenda. One of the ways was by assassination, and some of America's greatest leaders (e.g., Dr. Martin Luther King, President John F. Kennedy, Megar Evers, Robert Kennedy, Malcolm X, President Abraham Lincoln, and Harry and Harriette Moore) have been assassinated because their agendas differed from a particular king or queen's agenda and posed a threat to that leader's power structure.

Lastly, the third rook, the Supreme Court, started in 1789 with three people whose names were Jay, Rutledge, and Ellsworth. Today, the purpose of the Supreme Court is to be the final judge in all cases involving laws of Congress and the highest law of all:

---
18 https://www.cia.gov/index.html.

the Constitution. The Supreme Court, however, is far from all powerful. The other two branches of government limit its power.

The president nominates justices to the court.[19] The Supreme Court has eight justices who are appointed to serve for life; they will remain on the court unless they retire, die, resign, or are impeached.

Every nation has a rook or rooks to protect their kings' and queens' power structure, whether they obtained their power through evil or good means.

---

19 http://www.scholastic.com/teachers/article/role-supreme-court.

CHAPTER 3

The Bishops

• • •

THE FOLLOWING RELIGIONS ARE WHO I consider to be bishops because they make up the majority of the religious morality in America. The bishops have a way of promoting the king's ideas. If the king is trying to get a particular person into a political office—say, for example, the presidential office—the king will financially contribute to different religious organizations to influence the outcome of support for the person that the king is wanting to be in that presidential office. Religion in America has had the biggest effect on how and what the American people believe. America's common and largest religion is Christianity. Christianity makes up 70 percent of the religion in America. The pilgrims first brought Christianity over from Europe in the 1600s. In America, there are different types of Christianity. The first, largest, and most common is the Catholic Church. It has been estimated that Catholicism, or the Catholic Church, today has 50,873,000 followers. The Pope usually leads the Catholic Church. The second largest and most common is the Baptist Church. It is estimated today that the Baptist Church has 33,830,000 followers. The Baptist Church is also the most diverse of the churches. Baptists follow different principles and doctrines that they think are correct. There are many different types of Christian branches or churches that teach different versions of the religion of Christianity.

Mormonism

Mormonism is a relatively new religion in the world, founded by Joseph Smith in the mid-nineteenth century in the northeastern United States. The official name of this religion is the Church of Jesus Christ of Latter-day Saints (LDS). The Mormon Church has distinct beliefs and an interesting history. Mormons are increasing in numbers in America and elsewhere in the world. When Mormonism is compared to orthodox

Christianity, it seems that these religions have similarities and differences. Although the name "Jesus Christ" is found in the church's official title, Mormon beliefs don't adhere to some doctrines regarding the person and work of Christ as they are adhered to in Roman Catholicism, Eastern Orthodoxy, and Protestant Christianity. Mormons deny the Trinity and have additional sacred books that they hold high in esteem for establishing doctrine and right conduct, like the Book of Mormon. They have their fair share of controversies, such as issues related to racial equality and polygamy. The LDS Church has worked to overcome those issues, which sometimes serve to foster misunderstanding about what Mormons believe and practice today. Modern-day Mormonism is known for its family-centered churches, missionary efforts around the world, an elaborate temple in Salt Lake City, Utah, and for its well-known church members, such as former presidential candidate Mitt Romney. Mormonism further teaches that people were formerly spirits in heaven, created by God the Father. According to LDS doctrine, Jesus atoned for mankind's sin in the garden of Gethsemane when he sweated blood. Members of the LDS Church believe that people can be saved from sin and go to heaven in different ways according to the Mormon doctrine of salvation. The afterlife in Mormonism also has a unique teaching that is different from Christianity.

BAPTIST

Baptist is a Christian religion. The Baptists are one of the largest Christian denominations. As indicated by their name, the primary Baptist is distinctive in practice. Baptists are believers in baptism and but reject infant baptism. Most Baptists are evangelical in doctrine, but Baptist beliefs can vary due to the congregational governance system that gives autonomy to individual local Baptist churches. Historically, Baptists have played a key role in encouraging religious freedom and separation of church and state. In the United States, the two largest Baptist groups are the Southern Baptist Church and the American Baptist Church, with the former being the larger, which included Martin Luther King Jr., Charles Spurgeon, John Bunyan, and Billy Graham. At the turn of the twenty-first century, there were about 43,000,000 Baptists worldwide, with about 33,000,000 of those in the United States and 216,000 in Britain. There are over 850,000 Baptists in South America and 230,000 in Central America and the Caribbean.

ISLAM

Islam is monotheistic religion with over one billion followers. The faith is based on revelations received by the Prophet Muhammad in seventh-century Saudi Arabia. The Arabic word for "Islam" means "submission," reflecting the faith's central tenet of submitting to the will of God. Followers of Islam are called Muslims. According to Islamic tradition, the angel Gabriel appeared to the Prophet over the course of twenty years, revealing to him many messages from God. Muslims recognize some earlier Judeo-Christian prophets, including Moses and Jesus, as messengers of the same true God. But Muhammad is the last and greatest of the prophets, whose revelations alone are pure and uncorrupted, according to Muslims. Islamic practices center on the five pillars of Islam: faith, prayer, fasting, pilgrimage to Mecca, and several holidays and rituals. The prophet dedicated the remainder of his life to spreading a message of monotheism in the polytheistic world. In the year AD 622, he fled, but eight years later, Muhammad returned to Mecca with an army and conquered the city for Islam. Beginning after Muhammad's death, which occurred fifty years after he and his army conquered Mecca, the entire Islamic and Judeo-Christian population in the West have had a challenging relationship for centuries, and today's conflicts in the Middle East are religiously charged. Thus, a focus on the facts and efforts toward mutual understanding are particularly important when it comes to Islam.

Catholicism

Roman Catholicism did not begin at a specific point in history, as the Protestant denominations did. In its long history, the church has evolved into a distinctive branch of Christianity with beliefs, practices, and organization that differ from both Protestantism and Orthodoxy. Roman Catholicism is by far the largest Christian group. With more than one billion adherents, Catholics constitute about half of the world's Christians. Catholicism is the majority religion in Italy, Spain, and nearly all Latin American countries. In 2001, about 24 percent of Americans identified themselves as Catholic, making Catholicism the largest denomination in America. The next largest denomination is Baptist, which constitutes 16 percent of Americans. Yet if Protestants are considered as one group, Catholics remain a minority among America's Christians.

Roman Catholic beliefs do not differ drastically from those of Christianity, Greek Orthodoxy, and Protestantism. All three main branches hold to the doctrine of the Trinity, the divinity of Jesus Christ, the inspiration of the Bible, and so on. But in terms of more doctrinal points, there are distinctive Roman Catholic beliefs, which include the special authority of the Pope, the ability of saints to intercede on behalf of believers, the concept of purgatory as a place of afterlife purification before entering heaven, and the doctrine of transubstantiation—that the bread used in the Eucharist becomes the true body of Christ when blessed by a priest. All information gathered was from ReligionFacts.com

CHAPTER 4

The Knights

• • •

AFTER PLAYING A COUPLE OF games of chess with some of my friends during chess club at Alton High School on Wednesday, October 14, 2015, I thought about the knights. The knight piece in chess can move in an L-shaped direction, meaning it can go three spaces up, left, right, or down and then over one. The knight piece can go through the pawn walls, which started to make me think about how the police can have a search warrant which enables them to come into a home and search it. The pawns represent the middle class and the poor how they can be sacrificed by those higher above them. You might be asking yourself how the pawns can be sacrificed. That's a simple question to answer. The pawns are sacrificed through jobs, imprisonment, debt, racism, and so on. Below you will read about the role of knights in America and the various ways their role affects others.

The knights today are law enforcement officers including those upholding federal laws, state laws, and state constitutions, according to PoliceOne.com.[20] The knights in chess are the only chess piece that can bust through the wall. This is analogous to police being sent in to calm or suppress rioters or protesters. The knights can also be influential by going undercover to seek drug dealers or to find people who could cause trouble. Many cops do this so they can get more information about the people in the area or sometimes to calm people down by just dressing up like the people in the area.

As I was doing my research about the various types of knights, I came across this website: http://www.golawenforcement.com/TypesofLawEnforcementJobs2.htm.[21]

---

20 Policeone.com.
21 http://www.golawenforcement.com/TypesofLawEnforcementJobs2.htm.

I found out that knights could be on various local, state, and federal agency levels. For example, each state government maintains a department of justice responsible for the prosecution of crimes. Counties, cities, and towns also employ attorneys to prosecute crimes against state or local ordinances. These departments are staffed by attorneys, who present the government's evidence to a judge or jury for a final determination of guilt. Known as a county or city attorney, district attorney, commonwealth attorney, prosecutor, state's attorney, or deputy attorney general, these legal professionals are granted wide discretion with regard to deciding whether to prosecute, what charges to file, and whether to permit a plea agreement.

When conducting a grand-jury investigation, the prosecution of a crime begins well before the perpetrator is ever charged. In all but two states, a grand jury is convened prior to the issuance of an indictment or formal criminal charge. The prosecutor presents evidence in the form of witness testimony before the grand jury, whose members then decide whether there is probable cause for a criminal charge. Grand-jury proceedings are closed to the public and are not subject to the rules of evidence. As such, hearsay evidence and testimony otherwise inadmissible in a trial may be introduced to the grand jury. In most jurisdictions, grand juries are reserved for the indictment of felony crimes only.

The prosecutors are given wide discretion as they decide whether or not to prosecute an offender. Even if the evidence seems solid in the grand-jury proceedings, there is always the possibility that the evidence will not be enough to move forward—witnesses disappear, or evidence reveals that another perpetrator was actually responsible. Criminal charges stemming from a police investigation, as opposed to a grand jury, often present a prosecutor with the difficult choice of accepting the charges or declining to prosecute. Citizen complaints alleging criminal activity are often declined due to a lack of evidence.

The duties of a criminal attorney involve investigating evidence. If a prosecutor decides to go forward with a case, he or she must study and understand all of the evidence presented to ensure the evidence meets the elements of the crime. The state legislature defines each crime with a series of elements, all of which must be met to satisfy the state's burden of proof. It is the prosecutor's job to make certain the evidence available and admissible in the case is sufficient to meet this burden. The prosecutor generally relies on the police to produce sufficient evidence of the crime, but it is the prosecutor's ultimate responsibility to investigate illegal activity.

The prosecutor can offer plea bargains. Prosecutors are given wide discretion to negotiate with the defendant's attorney for a possible plea bargain. A plea bargain is when the state, through its prosecutor, agrees to charge the defendant with a lesser crime, carrying less penalty, in exchange for a waiver of the defendant's right to a trial. The prosecutor must present the plea agreement to the judge, who will review the new charges with the defendant and make certain he or she understands the agreement.

If a criminal case goes to trial, the prosecutor must first work with the defense attorney to select a jury to hear the case. The prosecutor must investigate the background of jurors for potential bias and may excuse any candidate who likely cannot render an impartial verdict. Once the jury is empaneled, the prosecutor presents the jury with an opening statement summarizing the case. The state presents its evidence first, followed by the defense. Throughout the trial, the prosecutor must make appropriate objections against evidence possibly inadmissible under the rules of evidence.

In regards to the litigation of appeals, In the event that the state loses its case, the prosecutor can appeal the case to the next highest state court. Many states employ appellate attorneys specifically for appeals. Appeals prosecutors review the evidence and records from the trial and form an oral argument before the appellate court. Appellate courts do not permit the introduction of new evidence and only allow each side approximately fifteen minutes to argue its position.

On the local, state, and federal agency levels, people depend on police officers and detectives to protect their lives and property. Law enforcement officers perform these duties in a variety of ways depending on the size and type of their organization. In most jurisdictions, they are expected to exercise authority when necessary, whether on or off duty.

There are three basic types of law enforcement jobs: uniformed officer, investigator, and support positions. All three types of law enforcement jobs are utilized at all three government levels of law enforcement agencies. Police and detectives held about 861,000 jobs in the United States in 2006. Local governments employed Seventy-nine percent. State police agencies employed about 11 percent, and various federal agencies employed about 7 percent. Local law enforcement agencies' police and detectives pursue and apprehend individuals who break the law and then issue citations or give warnings. Most police officers patrol their jurisdictions and investigate any suspicious activity they notice. Detectives, who are often called "agents" or "special agents," perform investigative duties such as gathering facts and collecting evidence.

The daily activities of police and detectives differ depending on their occupational specialty—such as police officer, game warden, or detective—and whether they are working for a local, state, or federal agency. Duties also differ substantially among various federal agencies, which enforce different aspects of the law. Regardless of job duties or location, police officers and detectives at all levels must write reports and maintain meticulous records that will be needed if they testify in court.

Sheriffs and deputy sheriffs enforce the law on the county level. Sheriffs are usually elected to their posts and perform duties similar to those of a local or county police chief. Sheriffs' departments tend to be relatively small, most having fewer than fifty sworn officers. Deputy sheriffs have law enforcement duties similar to those of officers in urban police departments. Police and sheriffs' deputies who provide security in city and county courts are sometimes called bailiffs.

Uniformed police officers have general law enforcement duties, including maintaining regular patrols and responding to calls for service. They may direct traffic at the scene of an accident, investigate a burglary, or give first aid to an accident victim. In large police departments, officers usually are assigned to a specific type of duty. Many urban police agencies are involved in community policing—a practice in which an officer builds relationships with the citizens of local neighborhoods and mobilizes the public to help fight crime. Uniformed officer jobs are those of a local police officer, deputy sheriff, state trooper, or a border patrol agent. These officers have an enforcement role. Agencies, which have uniformed officers, also have investigative divisions, such as the homicide division of a local police department or the narcotics division of a state trooper agency. While unformed officers may conduct investigations as part of their role, those in an investigative division may have a primary role of conducting criminal investigations. Officers move into these investigative positions through promotion and advancement. They are usually not hired directly to work in an investigation division.

Another type of knight, the detective, is a plain-clothes investigator who gathers facts and collects evidence for criminal cases. Some are assigned to task forces to combat specific types of crime. They conduct interviews, examine records, observe the activities of suspects, and participate in raids or arrests. Detectives and state and federal agents and inspectors usually specialize in investigating one type of violation, such as homicide or fraud. They are assigned cases on a rotating basis and work on them until an arrest and conviction is made or until the case is dropped.

There are agencies that conduct criminal investigations rather than uniformed enforcement. An example of this would be the US Drug Enforcement Administration, the FBI, or the Georgia Bureau of Investigation. These personnel are usually special agents and in work plain clothes. These agencies hire people directly to become special agents and conduct criminal investigations. Some agencies have a separate uniformed division and an investigative division, such as the Secret Service.

The state law enforcement agencies hire state police officers, sometimes called state troopers or highway patrol officers, who arrest criminals statewide and patrol highways to enforce motor vehicle laws and regulations. State police officers often issue traffic citations to motorists. At the scene of accidents, they may direct traffic, give first aid, and call for emergency equipment. They also write reports used to determine the cause of the accident. State police officers are frequently called upon to render assistance to other law enforcement agencies, especially those in rural areas or small towns. State law enforcement agencies operate in every state except Hawaii. Most full-time sworn personnel are uniformed officers who regularly patrol and respond to calls for service. Others work as investigators, perform court-related duties, or carry out administrative or other assignments.

When it comes to federal law enforcement agencies, the federal government works in many areas of law enforcement. Federal Bureau of Investigation (FBI) agents are the government's principal investigators, responsible for investigating violations of more than two hundred categories of federal law and conducting sensitive national security investigations. Agents may conduct surveillance, monitor court-authorized wiretaps, examine business records, investigate white-collar crime, or participate in sensitive undercover assignments. The FBI investigates a wide range of criminal activity, including organized crime, public corruption, financial crime, bank robbery, kidnapping, terrorism, espionage, drug trafficking, and cybercrime.

There are many other federal agencies that enforce particular types of laws. US Drug Enforcement Administration (DEA) agents enforce laws and regulations relating to illegal drugs. Deputy marshals and US marshals protect the Federal courts and ensure the effective operation of the judicial system. Agents of the Bureau of Alcohol, Tobacco, Firearms, and Explosives enforce and investigate violations of federal firearms and explosives laws, as well as federal alcohol and tobacco tax regulations. Special agents from the US Department of State Bureau of Diplomatic Security are engaged in the battle against terrorism.

The Department of Homeland Security also employs numerous law enforcement officers within several different agencies, including Customs and Border Protection, Immigration and Customs Enforcement, and the US Secret Service. US Border Patrol agents protect more than eight thousand miles of international land and water boundaries. Immigration inspectors interview and examine people seeking entrance to the United States and its territories. Customs inspectors enforce laws governing imports and exports by inspecting cargo, baggage, and articles worn or carried by people, vessels, vehicles, trains, and aircraft entering or leaving the United States. Federal air marshals provide air security by guarding against attacks targeting US aircraft, passengers, and crews. US Secret Service special agents and US Secret Service uniformed officers protect the president, vice president, their immediate families, and other public officials. Secret Service special agents also investigate counterfeiting, forgery of government checks or bonds, and fraudulent use of credit cards.

The jobs of some federal agents such as US Secret Service and DEA special agents require extensive travel, often on very short notice. They may relocate a number of times over the course of their careers. Some special agents in agencies such as the US Border Patrol work outdoors in rugged terrain for long periods and in all kinds of weather.

The working conditions of the police officers and detectives can be very challenging. They are required to work whenever they are needed and may work long hours during investigations. Most Officers in jurisdictions, whether on or off duty, are expected to be armed and to exercise their authority when necessary.

Another type of knight is the police patrol officer.[22] The police patrol officer is responsible for patrolling assigned areas in a police cruiser in search of suspicious activity such as prostitution, drug trafficking, speeding, driving under the influence, and other violations. The patrol officer arrests violators, books them in prison, and testifies in court proceedings. The following lists are the primary responsibilities of the police patrol officer:

Patrol area to protect people's lives and property.
Regulate traffic.
Respond to accidents or stranded motorists.
Identify and arrest people accused of violations, including assault, burglary, larceny, and carjacking.

---

22 http://www.americasjobexchange.com/police-patrol-officer-job-description.

Enforce motor vehicle laws.

Testify in court.

Bag and present the evidence.

Respond to distress calls or calls for assistance.

Investigate reports of suspicious activity.

Interview witnesses and suspects.

Call for backup if needed.

Pursue fleeing suspects on foot.

Search vehicles for drugs or paraphernalia.

Investigate traffic accidents to determine cause of accident.

Provide road assistance to motorists and give directions if necessary.

Assist transients with relocation and shelter information.

Book and process prisoners.

Write records of arrests and reasons for arrest.

Reroute traffic in case of accidents or emergencies.

Escort citizens during funeral processions.

Issue citations or warnings to people who violate motor vehicle laws.

Check for proper identification and verify licenses and registration during traffic stops.
Use drug dogs to search houses or vehicles for drugs.
Patrol areas on horseback.

Another type of knight is the probation and parole officer.[23] The probation and parole officer's basic purpose is to provide professional social service and law enforcement duties in the areas of assessment of criminogenic need, transition plan design, treatment referral, and ongoing monitoring of offender behavior. Supervision services are provided in the community for probationers, parolees, and inmates in reentry programs for the purpose of increasing public safety through the reduction of future criminal behavior. The functions within this family of jobs will vary by level, but may include the following: managing a caseload of adult felons by employing motivational interviewing skills to complete a scientific assessment of criminogenic risk/need and to determine the offender's stage of change for each identified need area; meeting the needs of each offender; referring offenders to appropriate treatment and/or programs to target the offender's primary

---

23 http://www.ok.gov/opm/jfd/i-specs/i40.htm.

criminogenic needs; monitoring activities of offenders to ensure adherence to action steps negotiated through transition planning and to conditions ordered by releasing authority; assisting offenders in obtaining and maintaining employment; engaging in ongoing support for the offender in the community by assisting the offender in identifying a network of family and friends with a prosocial orientation; and identifying prosocial interests and activities that are geared toward improving bonds and ties to prosocial community members.

Parole officers engage in the following:

- Conduct various investigations including, but not limited to, presentence, interstate, prepardon, and preparole investigations.
- Prepare reports concerning activities of offenders and provide recommendations for the use of the releasing authority.
- Maintain documentation, physical and electronic, relating to management of offender caseload.

- Monitor payment of financial obligations ordered by the releasing authority; collect and document offender payments.
- Assist in security operations in the event of a prison riot or disturbance; arrests and transports offenders when required.
- Conduct periodic screening for drug and alcohol use by offenders.

As you can imagine from all the information discussed above, the role that knights play in America is critical to helping protect others as well as the kings and queens, the top 1 percent.

CHAPTER 5

Pawn One: The Native Americans

• • •

IN THE UNITED STATES OF America, there are many different and unique ethnic groups. These ethnic groups have their history and unique cultures, which they have gotten from their ancestors and their ancestors' ancestors before them. But I'll start with the first people in America; the first people were the Native Americans.

Before I show you the statistical analysis of the Native Americans, I want to shed light on some of the ways America's chessboard comes into play. Whenever a society favors the top 1 percent, which are the kings and queens of America, the pawns always suffer, which causes them to be sacrificed, devalued, and unappreciated in every area that affects their lives. It affects their self-esteem, education, health, financial outcome, employment, housing, and even the type of food they can afford to purchase.

Native Americans came from northeast Asia. They journeyed over a land bridge between Siberia and Alaska some twelve thousand years ago and then migrated across North and South America.[24] Scientists have done DNA tests on the Native Americans, and their DNA was matched to DNA found in China, Mongolia, and Siberia.[25]

The Native Americans in America and Alaskan natives make up 2 percent of the population; there are 5.2 million in America. The majority of Native Americans live on their reservation where their tribe lives. The Cherokee tribe, for example, now lives in northeast Oklahoma on their reservation. The Native Americans who live on the reservations have their own government with their

---

24 http://news.nationalgeographic.com/.
25 http://www.cdc.gov/.

own laws and school systems with their own teachers. Like many people today in the United States, Native Americans struggle with unemployment, poverty, and discrimination.

According to the US Census Bureau, these Americans earn a median annual income of $33,627. One in every four (25.3 percent) lives in poverty, and nearly a third (29.9 percent) are without health insurance coverage.[26]

Native Americans suffer from the highest rates of diabetes of any ethnic group in the United States.[27] Other problems Native Americans face are injuries, sexual abuse, tuberculosis, and suicide.[28]

Statistics on Native Students

The following are demographics and statistics about our American Indian and Alaska Native (AI/AN) populations and students.

---

26 http://www.spotlightonpoverty.org/exclusivecommentary.aspx?id=0fe5c04e-fdbf-4718-980c-0373ba823da7#sthash.J8dSHWWV.dpuf.
27 http://www.pewresearch.org/.
28 http://america.aljazeera.com/.

Notes: "AI/AN" means American Indian and Alaska Native. "NHOPI" means Native Hawaiian and Other Pacific Islander. "Alone" means not in combination with any other race. "In combination" means in combination with at least one other race.

AI/AN Population (All Ages)

The U.S. Census Bureau's American Community Survey estimates that in 2012, there were 5,226,034 American Indian and Alaska Natives (alone or in combination), comprising 1.7 percent of the total U.S. population of 313.9 million. Among these AI/ANs, 2,563,505 (0.8 percent) were American Indian and Alaska Native alone and 2,288,331 (0.7 percent) were American Indian and Alaska Native in combination. (US Census Bureau, 2012 American Community Survey)

The population of AI/ANs, "(alone or in combination)" increased by 27 percent between 2000 and 2010, compared to the 10 percent increase among the overall U.S. population.

In 2012, the median age of American Indian and Alaska Natives (alone) was 31 years, compared to the median age of 37 years for the overall U.S. population. In 2012, the median income of American Indian and Alaska Native (alone) households was $35,310, compared to $51,371 for the entire nation.

In 2012, 29.1 percent of American Indian and Alaska Native (alone) lived in poverty—the highest rate of any race group—compared to 15.9 percent for the entire nation.

Greatest Numbers

In 2012, the 10 states projected to have the greatest number of American Indian and Alaska Native's (alone or in combination) were California (N=710,007), Oklahoma (511,353), Arizona (N=350,960), Texas (N=315,126),

New Mexico (N=216,225), Washington (N=204,438), New York (N=187,058), North Carolina (N=186,442), Florida (N=145,804), and Alaska (N=143,610). In 2010, the 10 cities with the greatest number of AI/ANs (alone or in combination) were New York, NY (111,749), Los Angeles, CA (54,236), Phoenix, AZ (43,724), Oklahoma City, OK (36,572), Anchorage, AK (36,062), Tulsa, OK (35,990), Albuquerque, NM (32,571), Chicago, IL (26,933), Houston, TX (25,521), and San Antonio, TX (20,137).

Greatest Percentages

In 2010, the 10 states projected to have the greatest percentage of American Indian and Alaska Native's (alone or in combination) were Alaska (19.6 percent), Oklahoma (13.4 percent), New Mexico (10.4 percent), South Dakota (10.0 percent), Montana (8.1 percent), North Dakota (6.4 percent), Arizona (5.4 percent), Wyoming (3.9 percent), Washington (3.0 percent), and Oregon (3.0 percent).

In 2010, the 10 cities with the greatest percentage of AI/ANs (alone or in combination) were Anchorage, AK (12 percent), Tulsa, OK (9 percent), Norman, OK, (8 percent), Oklahoma City, OK (6 percent), Billings, MT (6 percent), Albuquerque, NM (6 percent), Green Bay, WI (5 percent), Tacoma, WA (4 percent), Tempe, AZ (4 percent), and Tucson, AZ (4 percent). Tribes & Reservations

In 2010, there were 324 federally recognized American Indian reservations. In 2012, excluding Hawaiian Home Lands had 618 AI/AN legal, and statistical areas for which the Census Bureau provides statistics. As of January 2012, there were 566 federally recognized Indian tribes. In 2010, the 10 American Indian Reservations with the greatest numbers of AI/ANs were the Navajo Nation Reservation, AZ-NM-UT (169,321), Pine Ridge Reservation, SD-NE (16,906), Fort Apache Reservation, AZ (13,014), Gila River Indian Reservation, Arizona (11,251), Osage Reservation, Oklahoma (9,920), San Carlos Reservation, AZ (9,901), Rosebud Indian Reservation, South Dakota

(9,809), Tohono O'odham Nation Reservation, Arizona (9,278), Blackfeet Indian Reservation, Montana (9,149), and Flathead Reservation, Montana (9,138).

Student Demographics (K–12)

During the 2010–11 school year, there were 378,000 AI/AN (alone) students in the U.S. public school system, comprising 0.7 percent of the total public school population. NOTE: During the 2005–06 school year, there were 644,000 AI/AN students (alone or in combination) in the U.S. public school system, comprising 1 percent of the total public school population. The decrease between 2005–06 and 2010–11 is due in part to a requirement that schools now only count students as American Indian and Alaska Native's if they are AI/AN alone.

During the 2010–11 school year, there were 49,152 students in Bureau of Indian Education Schools.

Currently, the BIE oversees 183 elementary, secondary, residential, and peripheral dormitories in 23 states. During the 2011–12 school year, private school student enrollment was 0.5 percent for American Indian and Alaska Native (alone) students, compared to 71.2 percent for White (alone) students.

During the 2010–11 school year, the states in which American Indian and Alaska Native (alone) students comprised the greatest proportion of the total student population were: Alaska (20 percent), South Dakota (15 percent), New Mexico (11 percent), Montana, (10 percent), and Oklahoma (9 percent).

Between 2005 and 2011, the achievement gaps between American Indian and Alaska Native and non-AI/AN fourth graders and between American Indian and Alaska Native and non-AI/AN eighth graders did not change for reading, but increased for mathematics.

During the 2010–11 school year, 52 percent of American Indian and Alaska Native three, four, and five-year-olds were enrolled in part-day or full-day prep-rimary programs, compared to 67 percent of Whites (alone). In 2011, 52 percent of American Indian and Alaska Native (alone) children lived in two-parent households, compared to 75 percent of Whites (alone). In 2009, 19 percent of American Indian and Alaska Native 9th grade females received special education services, compared to the national rate of 7 percent for all 9th grade females, and 8 percent for White 9th grade females. In the same year, 27 percent of American Indian and Alaska Native 9th grade males received special education services, compared to the national average of 13 percent for all 9th grade males, and 13 percent for White males. During the 2008–09 school year 40 percent of American Indian and Alaska Native students attended a school that did not meet Adequate Yearly Progress, compared to 33 percent of White students.

During the 2007–08 school year, there were 741 public schools located in American Indian and Alaska Native areas, with 82,406 American Indian and Alaska Native students. In public schools with high American Indian and Alaska Native enrollment, only 16 percent of teachers are American Indian and Alaska Native Attendance & Discipline (K–12)

The 2009–10 out-of-school suspension rates for AI/AN females was 6 percent, compared to 3 percent for white females, and 12 percent for AI/AN males, compared to 7 percent for White males. School Crime & Safety (K–12)

In 2011, greater percentages of American Indian and Alaska Native students (40 percent) and NHOPI students (39 percent), than White, Black, or Asian students (23 percent each) reported that drugs were offered, sold, or given to them on school property.

In 2011, 47 percent of American Indian and Alaska Native and 31 percent of NHOPI (Native Hawaiian and Other Pacific Islander) students reported using marijuana anywhere, compared to 22 percent of White students.

In 2011, 8 percent of American Indian and Alaska Native and 11 percent of NHOPI 9th–12th grade students reported being threatened or injured with a weapon on school property at least once in a 12-month period, compared to 6 percent of white students.

In 2009–10, 13 percent of schools with less than 5 percent minority enrollment reported cyber-bullying among students, compared with 5 percent of schools with 50 percent or greater minority enrollment.

In 2011, 12 percent of American Indian and Alaska Native and 21 percent of NHOPI students reported being in a physical fight on school property during the previous 12 months, compared to 10 percent of White students.

In 2011, 42 percent of American Indian and Alaska Native and 43 percent of NHOPI students reported being in a physical fight anywhere during the previous 12 months, compared to 29 percent of white students.

In 2011, 28 percent of American Indian and Alaska Native and 21 percent of NHOPI students reported carrying a weapon anywhere in the previous 30 days, compared to 17 percent of white students.

In 2011, 21 percent of American Indian and Alaska Native students reported alcohol consumption on school property, compared to 4 percent of white students.

In 2011, 45 percent of American Indian and Alaska Native students reported consuming alcohol anywhere in the previous 30 days, compared to 40 percent of white students.[29]

God created the Native Americans, like all other ethnic groups, for a purpose and a reason. There is so much that has been learned and still can be learned and appreciated by valuing each ethnic group's unique talents and skills that have contributed to the creation of America.

---

29 http://www.niea.org/research/statistics.aspx.

CHAPTER 6

Pawn Two: The White Americans

• • •

THE WHITE AMERICANS ONCE WERE allies with the Native Americans, but soon after they became enemies in the early stages of America. In the past, some white Americans and Native Americans owned slaves. The history of the white Americans is old. The majority of their ancestors are Irish, English, Italian, Spanish, German, French, Norwegian, and Swedish. Some of the white American ancestors got to the United States in the 1600s on the Mayflower, which is how the pilgrims got here. Not all white Americans came to America as free people; some came to America as indentured servants.

The indentured servants weren't treated as horribly as the black American slaves were. The indentured servants were usually criminals, poor people, and debtors who had to pay off their debts. The length of time the indentured servants worked depended on the amount of their debt. According to the current US census definition,

"white" refers to a person having origins in any of the original peoples of Europe, the Middle East, or North Africa. It includes people who indicated their race as "white" or reported entries such as Irish, German, Italian, Lebanese, Arab, Moroccan, or Caucasian.

In US census documents, the designation White overlaps, as do all other official racial categories, with the term Hispanic or Latino, which was introduced in the 1980 census as a category of ethnicity, separate and independent of race. Hispanic and Latino Americans as a whole make up a racially diverse group and as a whole are the largest minority in the country. In cases where individuals do not self-identify, the US census parameters for race give each national origin a racial value.

Additionally, people who reported Muslim (or a sect of Islam such as Shi'ite or Sunni), Jewish, Zoroastrian, or Caucasian as their "race" in the "Some other race" section, without noting a country of origin, are automatically tallied as White. The US Census considers the write-in response of "Caucasian" or "Aryan" to be a synonym for White in their ancestry code listing.[30]

In 2010, the white Americans made up 72.4 percent of America, which was 223,553,265.

The following is income and educational attainment according to Wikipedia:

White Americans had the second highest median household income and personal income levels in the nation, by cultural background. The median income per household

---
30 https://en.wikipedia.org/wiki/White_American.

member was also the highest, since white Americans had the smallest households of any racial demographic in the nation. In 2006, the median individual income of a white American age twenty-five or older was $33,030, with those who were employed full-time and between ages twenty-five and sixty-four earning $34,432. Since 42 percent of all households had two income earners, the median household income was considerably higher than the median personal income, which was $48,554 in 2005. Jewish Americans ranked first in household income, personal income, and educational attainment among white Americans. In 2005, white households had a median household income of $48,977, which is 10.3 percent above the national median of $44,389. Among Cuban Americans, with 86 percent classifying as white, those persons born in the United States had a higher median income and educational attainment level than most other whites.

The poverty rates for White Americans are the second-lowest of any racial group, with 10.8 percent of white individuals living below the poverty line—3 percent lower than the national average. However, due to whites' majority status, 48 percent of Americans living in poverty are white.

Whites' educational attainment is the second-highest in the country, after Asian Americans'. Overall, nearly one-third of white Americans had a bachelor's degree, with the educational attainment for whites being higher for those born outside the United States: 37.6 percent of foreign born, and 29.7 percent of native born whites had a college degree. Both figures are above the national average of 27.2 percent.

Gender income inequality was the greatest among whites, with white men out earning white women by 48 percent. The Census Bureau data for 2005 reveals the median income of white females was lower than that of males of all races. In 2005, the median income for White females was only slightly higher than that of African American females.[31]

---

31 https://en.wikipedia.org/wiki/White_American.

White Americans, like all ethnic groups, have contributed to making America a great place to live. Every ethnic group should be valued and appreciated because we all need each other, and God created all humanity for a reason and a purpose.

CHAPTER 7

Pawn Three: The Hispanic Americans

• • •

THE HISPANICS ARE NOT REALLY a race of people at all. When most people think of the word "Hispanic," they think of a race of people instead of a nationality. What people need to understand is that there are many ethnic groups who hide their ethnicity under this label. You have the natives of the lands of Central America, the Caribbean islands, and South America. These natives are the people who would be described as indigenous by people; their ancestors have lived in these lands before Europeans and the African slaves came. They have their own culture, language, and history.

The Hispanics come from Asia, because their genetics and DNA links them to Asia.[32]

The next one is the European or white Hispanics whose ancestors originate from Europe. They either came to the Americas to start a new life, or they came to the Americas as colonists, like the Portuguese and Spanish. The white Hispanics mainly came to South America, Central America, the Caribbean Islands, and the southern parts of the United States.

The last Hispanic group would be the black Hispanics. The Afro-Hispanics were the ones—just like the black Americans and black English—who were sold from Africa to the four corners of the earth. The Afro-Hispanics were treated horribly as they came to the Americas on the slave ships. As they arrived, they were also stripped of their language, cultures, and history, just like the black Americans. Fortunately, they still kept little parts of their culture, even though it was stripped from them.

---

32 http://www.natureworldnews.com/articles/6011/20140213/dna-12-600-year-old-clovis-boy-shows-asians-ancestors.htm.

Hispanics are a mixture of different ethnic groups who came by free will or as slaves.

According to Wikipedia, the Hispanic population is forty million.

According to the US Bureau of the Census, the poverty rate among the six largest Hispanic groups during the period of 2007–2011 was as follows:

Dominican Americans (26.3 percent), Puerto Ricans (25.6), Guatemalan Americans (25.1), Mexican Americans (24.9 percent), Salvadoran Americans (18.9) and Cuban Americans (16.2). In comparison, the average poverty rates for non-Hispanic White Americans (10.8 percent) and Asian Americans (11.3 percent) were lower than those of any Hispanic group. African Americans (25.8 percent) had a higher poverty rate than Cuban Americans, Salvadoran Americans, Mexican Americans, Guatemalan Americans and Puerto Ricans, but had a lower poverty rate than Dominican Americans.[33]

---

33 https://en.wikipedia.org/wiki/Hispanic_and_Latino_Americans.

Workforce and Income

In 2011, the average individual income between Hispanic and Latino Americans was highest for Argentinian Americans ($55,000), and lowest for Honduran Americans ($31,000). For other large Hispanic groups the incomes were as follows: Salvadoran Americans ($40,000), Cuban Americans (38,600), Mexican Americans ($38,000), Guatemalan Americans ($36,400), Puerto Ricans ($36,000) and Dominican Americans ($32,300).

Among Hispanics, Cuban Americans (28.5 percent) had the highest percentage in professional-managerial occupations. The percentage for Mexican Americans was 20.7, Central and South Americans' was 8.8 percent, and Puerto Ricans was 7.2 percent. All these are lower than the average for non-Hispanics (36.2 percent).[34]

America's chessboard affects all ethnic groups. Everyone should be valued because all ethnic groups played a very important part

---
34 https://en.wikipedia.org/wiki/Hispanic_and_Latino_Americans.

in making America the great country that it is today. Every person in every ethnic group has a God-given purpose to be fulfilled on this earth. Every ethnic group needs to be appreciated and given the right to take advantage of every opportunity that is provided in America.

CHAPTER 8

Pawn Four: The Asian Americans

• • •

ASIAN AMERICANS ARE PEOPLE OF Asian descent who live in America. They may have come from places like Thailand, China, Laos, India, Mongolia, or Japan. These people have their own culture, history, and language. The earliest Asian Americans are known as the Native Indians of North America, South America, Central America, and the Caribbean Islands. However, the Asian Americans that we are more familiar with are those who came to America in the modern times. Their ancestors came to America sometime after the late 1800s. When they came to America, they had their fair share of racism and economic problems.

According to Wikipedia, Asian Americans started their own businesses because they were largely excluded from labor markets in the nineteenth century. They became very successful and influential in American society by starting businesses such as convenience and grocery stores, professional offices such as medical and law practices, laundromats, restaurants, beauty-related ventures, and high-tech companies.

They have dramatically expanded their involvement across the American economy. Asian Americans have been disproportionately successful in the technology sectors of California's Silicon Valley, as evidenced by the Goldsea 100 Compilation of America's Most Successful Asian Entrepreneurs.

Compared to their population base, Asian Americans today are well represented in the professional sector and tend to earn higher wages. The Goldsea compilation of Notable Asian American Professionals show that many have come to occupy high positions at leading US corporations, including a surprising number as Chief Marketing Officers.

Asian Americans have made major contributions to the American economy. In 2012, Asian Americans own 1.5 million businesses, employ around three million people who earn an annual total payroll of around $80 billion. Fashion designer and mogul, Vera Wang, who is famous for designing dresses for high-profile celebrities, started a clothing company, named after herself, which now offers a broad range of luxury fashion products. A. Wang founded Wang Laboratories in June 1951. Amar Bose founded the Bose Corporation in 1964. Charles Wang founded Computer Associates and later became its CEO and chairman. David Khym founded the hip-hop fashion giant, Southpole (clothing), in 1991. Jen-Hsun Huang co-founded the NVIDIA Corporation in 1993. Jerry Yang co-founded Yahoo! Inc.

in 1994 and became its CEO later. Andrea Jung serves as Chairman and CEO of Avon Products. Vinod Khosla was a founding CEO of Sun Microsystems and is a general partner of the prominent venture capital firm Kleiner Perkins Caufield & Byers. Steve Chen and Jawed Karim were co-creators of YouTube, and were beneficiaries of Google's $1.65 billion acquisition of that company in 2006. In addition to contributing greatly to other fields, Asian Americans have made considerable contributions in science and technology in the United States, in such prominent innovative R&D regions as Silicon Valley and The Triangle.[35]

Education

Among America's major racial categories, Asian Americans have the highest educational qualifications. This varies, however, for individual ethnic groups. Dr. C. N. Le, Director of the Asian & Asian American Studies Certificate Program at the University of Massachusetts, writes that although 42 percent of all Asian American adults

---
35 https://en.wikipedia.org/wiki/Asian_Americans.

have at least a college degree, Vietnamese Americans have a degree attainment rate of only 16 percent, while Laotians and Cambodians only have rates around 5 percent. It has been noted, however, that 2008 US Census statistics put the bachelor's degree attainment rate of Vietnamese Americans at 26 percent which is not very different from the rate of 27 percent for all Americans. According to the US Census Bureau in 2010, while the high school graduation rate for Asian Americans is on par with those of other ethnic groups, 50 percent of Asian Americans have attained at least a bachelor's degree as compared with the national average of 28 percent and 34 percent for non-Hispanic whites. Indian Americans have some of the highest education rates, with nearly 71 percent, having attained at least a bachelor's degree in 2010. According to Carolyn Chen, director of the Asian American Studies Program at Northwestern University, as of December 2012 Asian Americans made up 12–18 percent of the student population at Ivy League schools. For example, the Harvard Class of 2016 is 21 percent Asian American.

In the years immediately preceding 2012, 61 percent of Asian American adult immigrants had a bachelor's degree or a graduate degree.[36]

On the American chessboard, the Asian Americans have been major contributors in every aspect of America—from their talents and skills to the sustaining of their culture because of the close family relationships in their household. This is why I believe the Asian Americans have been especially successful in the business, education, and medical fields.

The Asian Americans have a God-given purpose and talent, which has contributed to making America great. They use their talents and skills in every aspect of their lives. It makes them stronger and enables them to survive as an ethnic group in America.

---

36 https://en.wikipedia.org/wiki/Asian_Americans.

CHAPTER 9

Pawn Five: The Afro-Americans

• • •

THE LAST ETHNIC GROUP IN America that I will talk about is the Afro-Americans. The Afro-Americans have suffered the worst crimes in history, from the transatlantic slave trade to the slave plantations of America. The ancestry of the Afro-Americans is a bit more confusing than the ancestry of the Native Americans, European Americans, and Asian Americans. The Afro-Americans have had their culture, language, history, and heritage stripped from them, and they were forced to forget it by the slave owners.

The first Afro-Americans came to this country in 1619 during the transatlantic slave trade, which ended in 1859.

Education

By 2012, Afro-Americans had advanced greatly in education attainment. They still lagged overall compared to white or Asian Americans but surpassed other ethnic minorities, with 19 percent earning bachelor's degrees and 6 percent earning advanced degrees. Between 1995 and 2009, freshmen college enrollment for African Americans increased by 73 percent, but had increased only 15 percent for whites. Predominantly black schools from kindergarten through twelfth grade students were common throughout the United States before the 1970s. By 1972, however, desegregation efforts meant that only 25 percent of black students were in schools with more than 90 percent non-white students. However, since then, a trend towards re-segregation has affected communities across the country. By 2011, 2.9 million African American students were in such overwhelmingly minority schools, including 53 percent of black students in school districts that were formerly under desegregation orders.

Historically black colleges and universities (HBCUs), which were originally set up as segregated colleges, continue to thrive and educate students today. The majority of HBCUs were established in the southeastern United States, with Alabama having the most HBCUs of any state.

As late as 1947, about one third of African Americans over sixty-five were considered illiterate, and were unable to read and write their own names. By 1969, illiteracy, as it had been traditionally defined, had been largely eradicated among younger African Americans.

US census surveys showed that by 1998, 89 percent of African Americans age twenty-five to twenty-nine had completed a high school education. Although this percentage is less than the percentage of whites or Asians who had completed high school, it was more than Hispanics. On many college entrance exams, standardized tests, and grades, African Americans have historically lagged behind whites, but some studies suggest that the achievement gap has been closing. Many policymakers have proposed that this gap can and will be eliminated through policies such as affirmative action, desegregation, and multiculturalism.

The average high school graduation rate of blacks in the United States has steadily increased to 71 percent in 2013. Separating this statistic into component parts shows it varies greatly depending upon the state and the school district examined. Thirty-eight percent of black males graduated in the state of New York, but in Maine 97 percent graduated and exceeded the white male graduation rate by 11 percentage points. In much of the southeastern United States, and in some parts of the southwestern United States, the graduation rate of white males was below 70 percent. For example, in Florida 62 percent of white males graduated from high school. Examining specific school districts paints an even more complex picture. In the Detroit school district, the graduation rate of black males was 20 percent, but it was 7 percent for white males. In the New York City school district, 28 percent of black males graduate high school compared to 57 percent of white males. In Newark County where 76 percent of black males graduated compared to 67 percent for white males.

In Chicago, Marva Collins, an African-American educator, created a low-cost private school specifically for the purpose of teaching low-income African-American children whom the public school system had labeled as being learning disabled. One article about Marva Collins' school stated,

"Working with students having the worst of backgrounds, those who were working far below grade level, and even those who had been labeled as "unteachable,"

Marva was able to overcome the obstacles. News of third grade students reading at ninth grade level, four-year-olds learning to read in only a few months, outstanding test scores, disappearance of behavioral problems, second-graders studying Shakespeare, and other incredible reports, astounded the public."

During the 2006–2007 school year, Collins' school charged $5,500 for tuition, and parents said that the school did a much better job than the Chicago public school system. Meanwhile, during the 2007–2008 year, Chicago public school officials claimed that their budget of $11,300 per student was not enough.[37]

Economic status

Afro-Americans have benefited from the advances made during the Civil Rights era, particularly among the educated, but not without the lingering effects of historical marginalization when considered as a whole. The

---
37 https://en.wikipedia.org/wiki/African_Americans.

racial disparity in poverty rates has narrowed. The black middle class has grown substantially. In 2010, 45 percent of African Americans owned their homes, compared to 67 percent of all Americans. The poverty rate among African Americans has decreased from 26.5 percent in 1998 to 24.7 percent in 2004, compared to 12.7 percent for all Americans. African Americans have a combined buying power of over $892 billion currently and likely over $1.1 trillion by 2012. In 2002, African American-owned businesses accounted for 1.2 million of the 23 million businesses in the United States. As of 2011 African American-owned businesses account for approximately 2 million US businesses. Black-owned businesses experienced the largest growth in number of businesses among minorities from 2002 to 2011.

In 2004, Afro-American men had the third-highest earnings of American minority groups after Asian Americans and non-Hispanic whites.

Twenty-five percent of blacks had white-collar occupations (management, professional, and related fields) in 2000, compared with 33.6 percent of Americans overall. In 2001, over half of African-American households of married couples earned $50,000 or more. Although in the same year African Americans were over-represented among the nation's poor, this was directly related to the disproportionate percentage of African-American families headed by single women; such families are collectively poorer, regardless of ethnicity.

In 2006, the median earnings of Afro-American men was more than black and non-black American women overall, and in all educational levels. At the same time, among American men, income disparities were significant; the median income of African-American men was approximately 76 cents for every dollar of their European American counterparts, although the gap narrowed somewhat with a rise in educational level.

Overall, the median earnings of Afro-American men were 72 cents for every dollar earned of their Asian American counterparts, and $1.17 for every dollar earned by Hispanic men. On the other hand, by 2006, among American women with post-secondary education, Afro-American women have made significant advances; the median income of Afro-American women was more than those of their Asian-, European- and Hispanic American counterparts with at least some college education.

The US public sector is the single most important source of employment for Afro-Americans. During 2008–2010, 21.2 percent of all black workers were public employees, compared with 16.3 percent of non-black workers. Both before and after the onset of the Great Recession, African Americans were 30 percent more likely than other workers to be employed in the public sector.

The public sector is also a critical source of decent-paying jobs for black Americans. For both men and women, the median wage earned by black employees is significantly higher in the public sector than in other industries.

In 1999, the median income of African American families was $33,255 compared to $53,356 of European Americans. In times of economic hardship for the nation, African Americans suffer disproportionately from job loss and underemployment, with the black underclass being hardest hit. The phrase "last hired and first fired" is reflected in the Bureau of Labor Statistics unemployment figures. Nationwide, the October 2008 unemployment rate for African Americans was 11.1 percent while the nationwide rate was 6.5 percent.

The income gap between black and white families is also significant. In 2005, employed blacks earned 65 percent of the wages of whites, down from 82 percent in 1975. The *New York Times* reported in 2006 that in Queens, New York, the median income among African American families exceeded that of white families, which the newspaper attributed to the growth in the number of two-parent black families. It noted that Queens was the only county with more than sixty-five thousand residents where that was true.

In 2011, it was reported that 72 percent of black babies were born to unwed mothers. The poverty rate among single-parent black families was 39.5 percent in 2005, according to Williams, while it was 9.9 percent among married-couple black families. Among white families, the respective rates were 26.4 percent.[38]

As an Afro-American young male, my perspective of the Afro-Americans is that they have had high points and low points. Afro-Americans have made major contributions to the development of America because without our free slave labor, America wouldn't have the status they have now. Afro-Americans built this country literally since we arrived in America as slaves, which gave other ethnic groups a major head start over the Afro-Americans.

Afro-Americans have a God-given purpose which is to be valued and appreciated. Despite all of the obstacles that were set

---
38 https://en.wikipedia.org/wiki/African_Americans.

before Afro-Americans, they rise up over and over again. Afro-Americans have a special God-given talent in many areas such art, education, sports, politics, medicine, and business, but more unity is needed within the Afro-American communities to rid themselves of crime and poverty. Afro-Americans need to improve in the areas of education and self-reliance; this is the only way to rid them of the cycle of poverty.

Religion also plays a very important part in the Afro-American communities across America. I feel that when Afro-Americans return back to their Hebrew heritage of faith and begin to start obeying the laws and commandments that Yah, the Most High Creator Elohim, gave to us by Moses according to the Book of Exodus at Mount Sinai (Hebrew: הר סיני, Har Sinai). Mount Sinai is the mountain where God gave the, *Ten Commandments* to Moses by God. Life will tremendously improve for Afro-Americans.[39]

---

39 https://en.wikipedia.org/wiki/Biblical_Mount_Sinai.

CHAPTER 10

The Overview

• • •

To MY READERS, I HOPE you have a better understanding of the analogy I used in my book *America's Chessboard*. My intentions were to bring a better understanding of the role each person plays in this chess game of life. All people living in America have a responsibility to live according to their divine purpose. Each chess piece affects the outcome of the other chess pieces. We are our brothers' keepers.

I hope the readers of my book find ways to affect other people in more positive ways. As the Bible (KJV) states in 1 Timothy 6:10, "For the love of money is the root of all evil: which while some coveted after, they have erred from the faith, and pierced themselves through with many sorrows."

When there is an opportunity to help or be kind to someone, I hope that you will show brotherly love toward your fellow human.

The Conclusion

• • •

THROUGHOUT THIS BOOK, YOU'VE READ about how the rich people in the first two chapters, the kings and queens, are really the rulers of this world. You learned about how the top 1 percent in America started their businesses and how they got to where they are now. You learned about the bishops and how they influence modern culture, such as the Roman Catholic Church. It gave birth to Christianity. The rooks are the FBI and the CIA. Their main purpose is to protect and defend America against terrorists and foreign-intelligence threats and to enforce laws in America. They also gather and analyze data and provide leadership and criminal justice services to federal, state, municipal, and international agencies. You also learned about how the knights are the military and law enforcement. The rich, who gave them authority, control the knights in this game. Lastly, you learned about the pawns, which are the middle class and poor in America.

The kings and queens are the ones who control America; and are the top 1 percent. The bishops help spread the doctrines that influence different religions. The rooks are the ones who carry out missions to destroy certain organizations that threaten the American people and their goals. The knights are the law enforcement officers who patrol the neighborhoods and keep watch for anything out of the ordinary.

Lastly, the pawns are all the ethnic groups that are in America. They are affected by being laid off, downsized, or terminated from their jobs.

America as a whole is a chessboard. In American society, everyone is playing against each other—the rich versus the poor and ethnicities versus other ethnicities—in an attempt to have the upper hand and get a checkmate. Now, let me say this to all, "My goal is for everyone to seek Yah (God) and his son,

Yahushua (Messiah) for these are the end days and everyone must prepare: Hebrews 9:27 - And as it is appointed unto men once to die, but after this the judgment: So all who reads this book check your hearts so that Yah (God) can save you in the end of Days, Shalom (Peace)!

Book Club Discussion and Topics

• • •

THE FOLLOWING GENERAL QUESTIONS WILL provide your book club with a great start in creating points for your discussions after you have read this work.

1. What was unique about the setting of the book?
2. How did the descriptions of the chess pieces enhance or take away from the story?
3. What specific themes did the author emphasize throughout this novel?
4. What do you think the author is trying to get across to his readers?

5. Can you relate to the characters' predicaments in this novel?
6. To what extent does anything in this work remind you of yourself, someone you know, or any of the actions you take?
7. How does any one of the chess pieces change or evolve throughout the course of the story?
8. What events initiated changes?
9. In what way do the events in this work reveal evidence of the author's views?
10. Did any parts of this book make you uncomfortable? If so, what?
11. Did this lead to a new understanding for you?
12. After reading this work, what awareness of any aspect of your life would you think about changing?

Notes

Notes

Notes

Notes

Notes

Notes

www.ingramcontent.com/pod-product-compliance
Lightning Source LLC
Chambersburg PA
CBHW032124090426
42743CB00007B/456